Captivating

Unveiling the Mystery of a Woman's Soul

The Couple's Guide

John and Stasi Eldredge

THOMAS NELSON
Since 1798

NASHVILLE DALLAS MEXICO CITY RIO DE JANEIRO BEIJING

Published in Nashville, Tennessee, by Thomas Nelson. Thomas Nelson is a trademark of Thomas Nelson, Inc.

Thomas Nelson, Inc., titles may be purchased in bulk for educational, business, fund-raising, or sales promotional use. For information, please e-mail SpecialMarkets@ThomasNelson.com.

ISBN 978-1-4002-8064-3

Printed in the United States of America

08 09 10 11 12 RRD 6 5 4 3 2 1

How to Use the Study Guides as a Couple

The messages in *Captivating* and *Wild at Heart* have helped millions of women and men discover the secret of the feminine and masculine hearts. Now, with the study guide you hold in your hand, that life-changing discovery is something you can share with your significant other. In the pages that follow you'll find questions, exercises, and journaling space that coordinate with *Captivating*.

Here's what we recommend for using this as a couple:

1) Read *Captivating* while your partner reads *Wild at Heart*.

2) After each chapter, process your experience and thoughts in this study guide.

3) Then, after you've both completed a chapter in your book and the corresponding study guide chapter, set some time aside to share with each other what you are learning, what discoveries you're making.

It's a simple process that will lead to a deep understanding of yourself *and* your partner. Without a doubt, you will both be astounded by the level of intimacy that can come from intentional sharing prompted by the message in these books!

Contents

Introduction

Welcome! Choosing to purchase this journal means that you are hungry for more. More of God, more healing, and more restoration into the woman you were created to be. It says that you are willing to take a journey of discovery *with him*. You have said "yes" to God. May he meet you in the deep places of your heart and bring you hope, courage, healing, and the delights of intimacy that only God can bring.

This is not your normal "workbook." There are no wrong answers. You don't have to struggle or worry about "getting it right." Besides, calling this a workbook would imply that the messages in the book *Captivating* are to be mastered. And mastered in a measurable way. Not at all. The messages in the book are to be pondered, considered. Some embraced. Some practiced. Some set aside for a later time.

This journal is for your heart. And words are the voice of the heart. Allow room for your heart to show up. Quiet yourself. Relax. Invite the Holy Spirit to guide you, speak to you, reveal what he desires to reveal.

The invitation is a true one. It is from God. And it is ever before you to come more fully into his presence and know him. Know yourself. And become ever more you, ever more his.

All of us are on a journey whether we know it or not. A journey of becoming. Henri Nouwen writes in *The Life of the Beloved* that "the spiritual life is not simply a way of being, but also a way of becoming." May God use this book in your life to aid you in becoming the woman you truly are. May he draw near to you as you draw near to him. Ask him to come. And rest assured that he will for, indeed, he has promised to do so; he delights in coming.

—Stasi Eldredge

The Heart of a Woman

You belong among the wildflowers
You belong in a boat out at sea
You belong with your love on your arm
You belong somewhere you feel free.

—TOM PETTY, "Wildflowers"

Welcome, Beloved of God. Take a deep breath. Relax. Before you pick up a pen, take a moment to invite Jesus into your time now; ask him to guide and lead and have his way with your thoughts and your heart. He is after all, the Creator of your heart, as a woman. And he knows the desires of your heart with intimate detail.

A WOMAN'S JOURNEY

Chapter 1 in the companion book retells the story of our Oxbow Bend canoeing experience; the beauty of it and the dangerous turn it took. Have you experienced something similar? Can you recall a time in your life when you felt *alive* as a woman? Who were you with? What happened? How did you feel?

When did you first know that you had become a woman, a "grown up"? Was there a milestone?

Do you feel that you *are* a woman? Are there places in your heart where you still feel young?

We know the expectations that have been laid upon us by our families, our churches, and our cultures. There are reams of materials on what you ought to do to be a good woman. But that is not the same thing as knowing what the journey toward becoming a woman involves, or even what the goal really should be. What expectations have been laid upon you, as a woman? What do you feel the pressure to be?

What have you been taught that a mature, godly woman should look like?

UNSEEN, UNSOUGHT, AND UNCERTAIN

I know I am not alone in this nagging sense of failing to measure up, a feeling of not being good enough as a woman. Every woman I've ever met feels it—something deeper than just the sense of failing at what she does. An underlying, gut feeling of failing at who she *is*. *I am not enough,* and *I am too much,* at the same time. Have you ever felt that way? Are you feeling it these days? In what ways?

The result is Shame, the universal companion of women. It haunts us, nipping at our heels, feeding on our deepest fear that we will end up abandoned and alone.

After all, if we were better women—whatever *that* means—life wouldn't be so hard. Right? Do you believe that? That if you were "better" life wouldn't be so hard? "Better" in what ways?

We long for intimacy and for adventure; we long to be the Beauty of some great story. But the desires set deep in our hearts seem like a luxury, granted only to those women who get their acts together. The message to the rest of us—whether from a driven culture or a driven church—is *try harder.* Do you resonate with that? Do you ever feel that way? How are you now "trying harder"?

THE HEART OF A WOMAN

And in all the exhortations we have missed the most important thing of all. We have missed the *heart* of a woman. And that is not a wise thing to do, for as the Scriptures tell us, the heart is central. "Above all else, guard your heart, for it is the wellspring of life" (Prov. 4:23 NKJV). Above all else.

Think about it: God created you as a woman. "God created man in his own image . . . male and female he created them" (Gen. 1:27). Whatever it means to bear God's image, you do so as a woman. Female. That's how and where you bear his image. Your feminine heart has been created with the greatest of all possible dignities—as a reflection of God's own heart. Is it a new thought to you that your heart as a woman is the most important thing about you? What does that mean to you?

TO BE ROMANCED

Listen to your own heart and the hearts of the women you know. We think you'll find that every woman in her heart of hearts longs for three things: to be romanced, to play an irreplaceable role in a great adventure, and to unveil beauty. Do you see those desires within your own heart? In your dreams? In your disappointments?

The desire to be romanced is set deep in the heart of every little girl and every woman. By looking at the stories we love, we can get a hint, a clue to what those desires are. What were some of your favorite stories or movies while you were growing up?

What are some of your favorite stories and movies now?

Do you want to be romanced? In what ways? (And if that desire seems faraway, or undesirable, ask yourself, "Why is that? When did I lose that desire?")

AN IRREPLACEABLE ROLE IN A GREAT ADVENTURE

Before doubt and accusation take hold, most little girls sense that they have a vital role to play; they want to believe there is something in them that is needed and needed desperately. Did you want to play a vital role in a great story?

What sort of adventures do you enjoy? And, do you enjoy them most by yourself or in sharing them with a close friend or loved one?

As echoes of the Trinity, we remember something. Made in the image of perfect relationship, we are relational to the core of our beings and filled with a desire for transcendent purpose. We long to be an irreplaceable part of a shared adventure. Does that ring true to you? Do you want this?

BEAUTY TO UNVEIL

According to Psalm 45:11, "The King is enthralled by your beauty." What would it feel like to know that Jesus, your King, is enthralled by your beauty?

Do you remember a time when you were young that you wanted to be beautiful? When you wanted others to find you beautiful?

All little girls want to be delighted in. Their young hearts intuitively want to know they are lovely. When you were young, and your young heart asked the question "Am I lovely?" how were you answered?

By those whose opinions matter to you, how do you think you would be answered today?

How would you describe your feelings toward your own beauty? Ambivalent? Hopeless? Content?

Who in your life is beautiful to you? Why?

Is it primarily because of their outward appearance, or is it more a matter of their heart?

Beauty is so important that we'll come back to it again and again in this book. For now, don't you recognize that a woman yearns to be seen and to be thought of as captivating? We desire to possess a beauty that is worth pursuing, worth fighting for, a beauty that is core to who we truly are. *We want beauty that can be seen; beauty that can be felt; beauty that affects others; a beauty all our own to unveil.*

Do you want this beauty?

This is key: The desire to be beautiful, to have a beauty all our own to unveil is not primarily about our looks. It is a desire to be captivating in the depths of who we are.

THE HEART OF A MAN

There are three core desires in the heart of every man as well. But they are uniquely masculine. For starters, every man wants a battle to fight. Men also long for adventure. Finally, every man longs for a beauty to rescue. (If you haven't read *Wild at Heart,* you really should. It will open your eyes into the world of men.) Have you seen that in the men you know? In your husband, brothers, friends, and sons?

And, how have you felt about those desires in men? Do you like them? Encourage them?

Now—can you see how the desires of a man's heart and the desires of a woman's heart were at least *meant* to fit beautifully together? A woman in the presence of a good man, a real man, loves being a woman. His strength allows her feminine heart to flourish. His pursuit draws out her beauty. And a man in the presence of a real woman loves being a man. Her beauty arouses him to play the man, draws out his strength. She inspires him to be a hero. As a woman, do you long to draw out the strength of a man?

By Way of the Heart

The longings God has written deep in your heart are telling you something essential about what it means to be a woman, and the life he meant for you to live. You can find that life. If you are willing to embark on a great adventure. Are you aware of your heart wanting more?

Quiet your soul now and talk to God:

Dearest God, You fashioned my heart within. You had your eye upon me before the foundation of the world. Would you please come again for me now and tenderly and firmly hold my heart? Awaken my desires. Restore them to me. Lead me into becoming the woman you created me to be, the woman I long to be. I will risk taking this journey with you . . . this journey into my heart, and into yours. I trust you. I love you. I need you. All this, and all the unspoken longings of my heart, I pray, in Jesus' name. Amen.

CHAPTER 2

What Eve Alone Can Tell

Even to see her walk across the room is a liberal education.

—C. S. LEWIS

The creation story culminates with the creation of Eve. Eve is not an afterthought, not an appendage. Rather, she is the pinnacle, the crown of creation. Women bear the image of God in unique, essential, strong, and breathtaking ways. The core desires of a woman's heart are the very ways that she bears God's image. They reflect God's core desires as well. So dear heart, image bearer of a beautiful God, take a deep breath and invite Jesus in.

THE LOST PRINCESS

I was intrigued and enamored by Princess Anastasia. I felt a kinship with this mysterious princess, a connection to her—something deep in my heart whispered that I, too, was more than met the eye. Perhaps I, too, was a part of royalty, but my position had been lost. My heart quickened at the thought of being a woman who was once a true princess. I don't think I'm alone in this. Have you ever wondered why the Cinderella story keeps haunting us? Why is this notion of a hidden princess (and a prince who comes to find her) so enduring? Is there something in our hearts that is trying to speak to us? Who have you dreamed of being?

The desire of a woman's heart and the realities of a woman's life seem an ocean apart. Oh, we long for romance and an irreplaceable role in a great story; we long for beauty. But that's not the life we have. The result is a sense of shame. Is this true of you?

The great emptiness we feel points to the great place we were created for. Have you ever thought of your struggles and longings as pointing to something great that you are designed to be?

THE CROWN OF CREATION

Creation itself is a great work of art, and all works after it are echoes of the original. How it unfolded and where it reached its climax are mysteries worth unveiling. We will never truly understand women until we understand this. What are some of your favorite places of natural beauty?

It is worth noting here the glorious intimacy of man's creation. All the rest of God's masterpiece sprang into being merely from God speaking it to be. "Then God spoke . . ." But when it came time for God to create his image bearers, he *formed* them with his own hands. He breathed life into them himself. What do you think about that?

It is nearing the end of the sixth day, the end of the Creator's great labor, as Adam steps forth, the image of God, the triumph of his work. He alone is pronounced the son of God. Truly the masterpiece seems complete. And yet, the Master says that something is not good, not right. Something is missing—and that something is Eve. To make clear the point, what did God create last? Who is the final, astonishing work of God?

She is the crescendo, the final, astonishing work of God. Woman. Given the way creation unfolds, how it builds to ever higher and higher works of art, can there be any doubt that Eve is the crown of creation? Not an afterthought.

She fills a place in the world nothing and no one else can fill. Step to a window, ladies, if you can. Better still, find some place with a view. Look out across the earth and say to yourself, "The whole, vast world is incomplete without me. Creation reached its zenith in me." How does that feel to you? Can you even do it? Ask God to reveal to you if this is true.

WHAT DOES EVE SPEAK TO US?

The story of Eve holds such rich treasures for us to discover. The essence and purpose of woman is unveiled here in the story of her creation. She has a crucial role to play, a destiny of her own.

And she, too, bears the image of God. But in a way that only the feminine can speak. What can we learn from her? God wanted to reveal something about himself, so he gave us Eve. When you are with a woman, ask yourself, *What is she telling me about God?*

ROMANCE AND RELATIONSHIPS: THE ANSWER TO LONELINESS

The world is young and completely unstained. Adam is yet in his innocence and full of glory. He walks with God. Nothing stands between them. They share something none of us has ever known—only longed for: an unbroken friendship, untouched by sin. Yet something is not good? Something is missing? What could it possibly be? Eve. Woman. Femininity. Wow. Talk about significance. Have you thought about being a woman in this way? What would it do for your heart to embrace this truth?

What was "not good" was the fact that the man was "alone." "It is not good for the human to be alone; I shall make him a sustainer beside him." How true this is. Whatever else we know about women, we know they are relational creatures to their core. What occupies most of your concerns? Are they relationships, people, loved ones?

Most women *define* themselves in terms of their relationships, and the quality they deem those relationships to have. I am a mother, a sister, a daughter, a friend. Or, I am alone. This is not a weakness in women—it is a glory. A glory that reflects the heart of God. How *do* you define yourself?

GOD'S HEART FOR RELATIONSHIP

The vast desire and capacity a woman has for intimate relationships tells us of God's vast desire and capacity for intimate relationships. In fact, this may be the most important thing we ever learn about God—that he yearns for relationship with us. The whole story of the Bible is a love story between God and his people. He cares. He has a tender heart. Have you seen God as yearning for you? As longing to be loved *by you*?

Life changes dramatically when romance comes into our lives. Christianity changes dramatically when we discover that it, too, is a great romance. That God yearns to share a life of beauty, intimacy, and adventure with us. "I have loved you with an everlasting love" (Jer. 31:3 NKJV). Eve—God's message to the world in feminine form—invites us to romance. Through her God makes romance a priority of the universe. I think most women are a little embarrassed by their deep longings to be romanced. Are you? Is this something you openly share with others?

How does it change the way you feel about your own heart's desires to hear that through Eve God makes romance a priority of the universe?

God endows Woman with certain qualities that are essential to relationship, qualities that speak of God. She is inviting. She is vulnerable. She is tender. She embodies mercy. She is also fierce and fiercely devoted. A woman's righteous jealousy speaks of the jealousy of God for us. How are you doing on these qualities these days?

Do you feel as though you've been keeping relationship a high priority? What would you want to do to make it more central to your life—and the lives of those you love?

AN ADVENTURE TO SHARE

While Eve has a glory for relationship, that is *not* all she is essential for. Back in Genesis, when God sets his image bearers on the earth, he gives them their mission. Call it the Human Mission—to be all and do all God sent us here to do. The mission to be fruitful and conquer and hold sway is given *both* to Adam *and* to Eve. "And God said to *them* . . ." (Gen. 1:28 NKJV). Eve is standing right there when God gives the world over to us. She has a vital role to play; she is a partner in this great adventure. All that human beings were intended to do here on earth . . . we were intended to do *together*. Is this a new thought for you? How does it make you feel?

When God creates Eve, he calls her an *ezer kenegdo*. "It is not good that man should be alone; I will make him a [*ezer kenegdo*]" (Gen. 2:18 NKJV). Hebrew scholar Robert Alter, who has spent years translating the book of Genesis, says that this phrase is "notoriously difficult to translate." The various attempts we have in English are "helper" or "companion" or the notorious "help meet." Alter is getting close when it translates it "sustainer beside him." The word *ezer* is used only twenty other places in the entire Old Testament. And in every other instance the person being described is God himself, when you *desperately* need him to come through for you.

Most of the contexts are life and death, by the way, and God is your only hope. Your *ezer*. If he is not there beside you, you are dead. A better translation, therefore, of *ezer* would be "life-saver." *Kenegdo* means alongside, or opposite to, a counterpart. You see, the life God calls us to is not a safe life. God calls us to a life involving frequent risks and many dangers. Why else would we need him to be our *ezer*?

You are an *ezer*. A life-saver. Let that be true. How does it change the way you look at yourself? Does it elevate the role of woman?

That longing in the heart of a woman to share life together as a great adventure—that comes straight from the heart of God, who also longs for this. Women are endowed with fierce devotion, an ability to suffer great hardships, a vision to make the world a better place. How does your heart respond?

BEAUTY TO UNVEIL

That we even need to explain how beauty is so *absolutely essential* to God only shows how dull we have grown to him, to the world in which we live, and to Eve. Beauty is the essence of God. The first way we know this is through nature, the world God has given us. . . . Nature is not primarily functional. It is primarily *beautiful*. Which is to say, beauty is in and of itself a great and glorious good, something we need in large and daily doses (for our God has seen fit to arrange for this). What does this stir in you?

WHY BEAUTY MATTERS

Beauty is powerful. It may be the most powerful thing on earth. It is dangerous. Because it *matters*. Does beauty matter to you? In your home? In your appearance? In others?

FIRST, BEAUTY *SPEAKS.*

I sit outside on a summer evening and just listen and behold and drink it all in, and my heart begins to quiet, and peace begins to come into my soul. My heart tells me that "All will be well," as Julian of Norwich concluded, "And all manner of things will be well." That is what beauty says: *All shall be well.* What does your heart feel when you come into a spacious, lovely place?

Being with a woman who is at rest, a woman comfortable within her own beauty, is an enjoyable experience. She is trusting God, not *striving to become* beautiful, but allowing his beauty to more fully inhabit her. Have you had the experience of being with a woman who was stressed, striving, worried? Have you had the pleasure of being with a woman who is resting in God and knowing that all will be well? How did you feel around those women? What kind of woman do you tend to be?

BEAUTY ALSO *INVITES*

Recall what it is like to hear a truly beautiful piece of music. It captures you; you want to sit down and just drink it in. The same is true of a beautiful garden, or a scene in nature. You want to enter in, explore, partake of it, feast upon it. We describe a great book as "captivating." You can't wait to get back to it, spend time with it. All of the responses that God wants of us. All of the responses a woman wants, too. Would the friends who know you well describe you as an inviting woman? Why did you answer the way you did?

Beauty *nourishes*. It is a kind of food our souls crave. Have you been nourished by beauty?

Beauty *comforts*. There is something profoundly healing about it. Have you been comforted by beauty?

Beauty *inspires*. Think of what it might have been like to have been in the presence of a woman like Mother Teresa. Her life was so beautiful, and it called us to something higher. Think of the women that inspire you: what is it about their lives that calls you to something more?

Beauty is *transcendent*. It is our most immediate experience of the eternal.
. . . Sometimes the beauty is so deep it pierces us with longing. For what?
For life as it was meant to be. Beauty reminds us of an Eden we have never
known, but somehow know our hearts were created for. When has an
experience of beauty pierced you with longing? Can you describe it?

Beauty is, without question, the most *essential* and most *misunderstood*
of all of God's qualities—of all feminine qualities, too. We know it has
caused untold pain in the lives of women. But even there something is
speaking. Why so much heartache over beauty? . . . Women ache over the
issue of beauty—they ache to be beautiful, to believe they are beautiful,
and they worry over keeping it if ever they can find it. Okay—let your
heart speak about the ache. What does this whole subject of beauty stir in
you, in the way of an ache? And why?

But Why a Beauty to *Unveil*?

One of the deepest ways a woman bears the image of God is in her
mystery. By mystery we don't mean "forever beyond your knowing," but
"something to be explored." God yearns to be known, but he wants to be
sought after by those who would know him. He says, "You will find Me

when you search Me with all your heart" (Jer. 29:13 NKJV). Are you aware of this yearning, as a woman? And *are* you being sought after these days?

Whatever else it means to be feminine, it is depth and mystery and complexity, with beauty as their very essence. Now, lest despair set in, let us say as clearly as we can: Every woman has beauty to unveil. Every woman.

Because she bears the image of God. She doesn't have to conjure it, go get it from a salon, have plastic surgery or a breast implant. No, beauty is an *essence* that is given to every woman at her creation. What if this really *is* true about you—that you *are* a captivating woman? Let your heart go there for a moment; what does it bring?

Now take time to offer this prayer:

O Jesus, come into this place in my heart. Help me to believe that you have given me your beauty. That I am a woman through and through, and because of your creation in me, I, too, have a heart for romance, I, too, am a life-saver, and I do have beauty to offer the world. I ask this in your name. Amen.

CHAPTER 3

Haunted by a Question

O most pernicious woman!

—WILLIAM SHAKESPEARE

The fall of Eve is felt every day of our lives. We experience it at the hands of other women, and we grieve it in our own souls. We live a life marred by fallenness; things break, laundry never ends, monotony weighs us down, and on any given day sin rises up out of our flesh when we least expect it. We respond with quick anger. We don't tell the whole truth. Once again we are exposed as not being all that we were made to be, all that we long to be.

The grocery store story at the beginning of the companion chapter is meant to highlight the fact that our fallenness reveals itself in the everyday matters of life. How we drive. What we say. What we don't say. How we experience others.

Before we go any further, however, let us turn the gaze of our souls to our God. He knows us. He sees it all. And he returns our gaze with a heart full of love and with mercy in his eyes.

We talk about two basic ways in which women are fallen: either they become dominating and controlling, or desolate and clingy. Would you say you lean more toward being a controlling woman or a desolate woman?

25

What's Happened to Us?

Eve was given to the world as the incarnation of a beautiful, captivating God—a life-offering, life-saving lover, a relational specialist, full of tender mercy and hope. Yes, she brought a strength to the world, but not a striving, sharp-edged strength. She was inviting, alluring, captivating. Is that how you experience the women you know? Is that how people experience you?

Why do so few women have anything close to a life of romance? Loneliness and emptiness are far more common themes—so entirely common that most women buried their longings for romance long ago and are living now merely to survive. And it's not just romance—why are most of the relationships of women fraught with hardship? Even when relationships are good, it's never enough. Are you aware of loneliness deep within your heart?

And women are tired. We are drained. But it's not from a life of shared adventures. No, the weariness of women comes from lives that are crammed with routine, with chores, with hundreds of demands. Somehow, somewhere between our youth and yesterday, *efficiency* has taken the place of adventure. Most women do not feel they are playing an irreplaceable role in a great Story. At some level, do you feel like a hamster on a wheel—running, running? Are you busy? Are you tired?

A WOMAN'S DEEPEST QUESTION

Most women doubt very much that they have any genuine beauty to unveil. It is, in fact, our deepest doubt. When it comes to the issues surrounding beauty, we vacillate between striving and resignation. Work out, work on your life, try this discipline or that new program for self-improvement. Oh, forget it. Who cares anyway? Put up a shield and get on with life. Hide. Hide in busyness, hide in church activities, hide in depression. There is nothing captivating about me. Are you aware of the ways in which you hide?

Every woman in the core of her being is haunted by Eve. She knows, if only when she passes a mirror, that she is not what she was meant to be. Remembering the glory that was once ours awakens my heart to an ache that has long gone unfulfilled. Are you aware of your own beauty? (You possess it, dear one. You do.)

Little girls want to know, *Am I lovely?* The twirling skirts, the dress-up, the longing to be pretty and to be seen—that is what it's all about. We are seeking an answer to our Question. Is that the first time you've heard that core Question, "Am I lovely?" put into words? Are you aware that it *is* a woman's core question?

As we enter into an honest look at how we—like Eve—are not what we were meant to be, that we, too, have fallen, we do so under the banner of God's love. We do so knowing that we are under no condemnation—Jesus has taken care of our every sin.

When the world was young and we were innocent—both man and woman—we were "naked and unashamed" (Gen. 2:25). Nothing to hide. Simply . . . glorious. And while that world was young and we, too, were young and beautiful and full of life, a corner was turned. . . .

We fell.

The woman was convinced that God was holding out on her. Convinced she could not trust his heart toward her. In order to have the life she believed she needed, she was convinced she must take matters into her own hands. And so she did. Look into your own heart. Ask God to gently show you where you have this tendency as well.

Eve failed as Adam's *ezer kenegdo*. Rather than bringing him life, she invited him to his death. And Adam failed Eve as well. He offered not his strength but his silence; not his protection but his passivity. Have you seen this played out in your life? Seen it this week? Last night?

THE CURSE

To the woman he said,

> "I will greatly increase your pains in childbearing;
>> with pain you will give birth to children.
> Your desire will be for your husband,
>> and he will rule over you."

To Adam he said,

> "Because you listened to your wife and ate from
>> the tree about which I commanded you,
>>> 'You must not eat of it,'
> "Cursed is the ground because of you;
>> through painful toil you will eat of it
>> all the days of your life.
> It will produce thorns and thistles for you."
>> —Genesis 3:16–18

The curse on Adam cannot be limited only to actual thorns and thistles. If that were so, then every man who chooses not to be a farmer gets to escape the curse. No, the meaning is deeper, and the implications are for every son of Adam. Man is cursed with futility and failure. Life is going to be hard for a man now, in the place he will feel it most. Failure is a man's worst fear.

The curse for Eve and all her daughters cannot be limited only to babies and marriage, for if that were true then every single woman without children gets to escape the curse. Not so. The meaning is deeper, and the implications are for every daughter of Eve. Woman is cursed with loneliness (relational heartache), with the urge to control (especially her man), and with the dominance of men. What are your deepest heartaches? Your deepest worries?

Do you see the relational aspects of your sorrow?

Did you think it was just you? Something fundamentally and uniquely wrong with you?

When a woman falls from grace, what is most deeply marred is her tender vulnerability, beauty that invites to life. She becomes a dominating, controlling woman, a desolate, needy, mousy woman, or some odd combination of both.

DOMINATING WOMEN

Fallen Eve controls her relationships. She refuses to be vulnerable. And if she cannot secure her relationships, then she kills her heart's longing for intimacy so that she will be safe and in control. How this plays out over the course of her life, and how the wounds of her childhood shape her heart's convictions are often a complex story, one worth knowing. But beneath it all, behind it all, is a simple truth: Women dominate and control because they fear their vulnerability. Far from God and far from Eden, it seems a perfectly reasonable way to live. In what ways are you a controlling, dominating woman?

Would your children, your husband, or your friends and coworkers say you are controlling?

Controlling women tend to be very well rewarded in this fallen world of ours. We are the ones to receive corporate promotions. We are the ones put in charge of our women's ministries. "Can do, Bottom Line, Get-It-Done" kinds of women. In what ways have *you* been rewarded for being this kind of woman?

Are you comfortable trusting your well-being to someone else?

Do you see that this self-protective strategy of behavior stems from fear? Does that help you have more mercy for yourself? For others?

DESOLATE WOMEN

If on the one side of the spectrum we find that Fallen Eve becomes hard, rigid, and controlling, then on the other side you find women who are desolate, needy, far *too* vulnerable. Desolate women are ruled by the aching abyss within them. These are the women who buy books like *Men Who Hate Women and the Women Who Love Them* and *Women Who Love Too Much* and *Co-dependent No More*. They are consumed by a hunger for relationship. Are there times when this would describe you? In what ways?

Like Eve after she tasted the forbidden fruit, we women hide. We hide behind our make-up. We hide behind our humor. We hide with angry silences and punishing withdrawals. We hide our truest selves and offer only what we believe is wanted, what is safe. What is there about *you* that you would like to keep hidden from the eyes of those around you?

If they saw what you are trying to hide, what are you afraid their response would be?

What would it be like to ask those you love and live with, what you are like to live with? Too risky? Pray about it. It can be a very scary thing to do but also a very enlightening thing as well.

Indulging

Whether we tend to dominate and control, or withdraw in our desolation and hide, still . . . the ache remains. The deep longings in our heart as a woman just won't go away. And so we indulge.

We buy ourselves something nice when we aren't feeling appreciated. We "allow" ourselves a second helping of ice cream or a Super-Sized something when we were lonely. Romance novels (a billion-dollar industry), soap operas, talk shows, gossip, the myriads of women's magazines all feed an inner life of relational dreaming and voyeurism that substitutes—for a while—for the real thing. But none of these really satisfy, and so we find ourselves trying to fill the remaining emptiness with our little indulgences.

It is our insatiable need for more that drives us to our God. What we need to see is that all our controlling and our hiding, all our indulging, actually serves to separate us from our hearts. We lose touch with those longings that make us a woman. And they never, ever resolve the deeper issue of our souls.

What are some ways you indulge your heart? Where do you go instead of to God when the ache of your heart begins to make itself known?

Eve's Lingering Fear

Every woman knows now that she is not what she was meant to be. And she fears that soon it will be known—if it hasn't already been discovered—

and that she will be abandoned. Left alone to die a death of the heart. That is a woman's worst fear—abandonment. Underneath, in the deepest recesses of your heart . . . is this fear there?

Down in the depths of our hearts, our Question remains. Unanswered. We live haunted by that Question yet unaware that it still needs an answer. Close your journaling time with this prayer:

Dear God, merciful God. I need your help. Please forgive me for the ways that I choose to live that have nothing to do with trusting you. Please come for me. Reveal to me the ways that I live that are not pleasing to you and grant me the grace of a deep and true repentance. Please speak to my deep heart where I need to hear from you. How do you see me? Am I lovely to you? I give you permission to have your way with me. Reveal to me more of who you are, God, and who I am to you. Thank you. In Jesus' name. Amen.

CHAPTER 4

Wounded

Ah, Women, that you should be moving
here, among us, grief-filled,
no more protected than we are.

—RAINER MARIA RILKE

We opened this chapter in the companion book by telling the story of little Carrie's marvelous sixth birthday and how she was surrounded by parents who loved her deeply, intentionally, and well. She was a little girl who felt wanted and delighted in, cherished by both her mother and her father. Although the story is based on real people with real lives, to many of us, it sounds like a fairy tale. How did you feel reading about Carrie's birthday morning? Cynical? Longing?

Before you move into this chapter, ask Jesus to come.

MOTHERS, FATHERS, AND THEIR DAUGHTERS

The way you see yourself now, as a grown woman, was shaped early in your life, in the years when you were a little girl. We learned what it meant to be feminine—and if we were feminine—while we were very young. Women learn from their mothers what it means to be a woman, and from their fathers the value that a woman has. If a woman is comfortable with her own femininity, her beauty, her strength, then the chances are good that her daughter will be, too. Was your mother comfortable with her femininity? How would you describe her, as a woman?

Try to put some words to what you learned about femininity from watching your mother.

What did your father value about women? What did you learn from him about femininity?

MOTHER WOUNDS

Fallen women tend to sin in one of two ways. Either they become controlling, dominating women, or they become mousy, desolate women. Which way would you say your mother tended to sway? What was that like for you?

FATHER WOUNDS

All little girls want to know if they are delighted in, lovely, wanted. And their question is primarily answered by their father, or if he is absent, by his absence or by other key men in her life. Did your father delight in you? (And I mean in honorable, appropriate ways.) If he did, what about you did he delight in? How did you know it?

How did your father answer your Question, *"Am I captivating?"*

Is there a defining wound you remember receiving from your father or your mother? What happened?

Fallen men tend to sin in one of two ways. Either they become driven, violent men—their strength gone bad—or they become passive, silent men (like Adam)—their strength gone away. Which way would you say your father tended to sway? What was that like for you? Any specific memories?

THE MESSAGES OF OUR WOUNDS—AND HOW THEY SHAPED US

The wounds that we received as young girls did not come alone. They brought messages with them that struck at the core of our hearts, right in the place of our Question. *Our wounds strike at the core of our femininity.* The damage done to our feminine hearts through the wounds we received is made much worse by the horrible things we believe about ourselves as a result. What do you believe about yourself *as a woman?*

Many of us women feel that, as women, somehow we are not enough. We can't put words to it, but deep down we fear there is something terribly wrong with us. If we had been the princess, then our prince would have come. Do you feel that way? Believe that there is something at your very core that is wrong with you?

You see, the wounds we received did not come alone. They came with messages that were delivered with such pain we believed the messages were true. The vows we make as children are very understandable—and very, very damaging. They shut our hearts down. They are essentially a deep-seated agreement with the messages of our wounds. How did the wounds you received as a little girl shape the way you see yourself as a woman now?

What vows did you make on how you would live? (Ask for God's help. These things run so deeply inside of us they are difficult to see.)

SHAME

The result of the wounds we received was to make us believe that some part of us, maybe every part of us, is marred. Shame enters in and makes its crippling home deep within our hearts. Shame makes us feel, no, believe, that we do not measure up—not to the world's standards, the church's standards, or our own. Shame causes us to hide. "I was afraid because I was naked; so I hid" (Gen. 3:10). In what ways are you aware of that you are hiding these days?

AN UNHOLY ALLIANCE

The wounds we received and the messages they brought formed a sort of unholy alliance with our fallen nature as women. From Eve we received a deep mistrust in the heart of God toward us. Clearly, he's holding out on us. We'll just have to arrange for the life we want. We will control our world. But there is also an ache deep within, an ache for intimacy and for life. We'll have to find a way to fill it. A way that does not require us to trust anyone, especially God. A way that will not require vulnerability. In some ways, this is every little girl's story, here in this world east of Eden. Are you aware of a mistrust of God deep in your heart?

Are there times when you feel an ache and a longing for more intimacy and more life? (That's good, by the way.)

God has much more freedom to move within us when we are honest with him and with ourselves. But let's recognize together that we don't stop getting wounded once we grow up. In fact, some of our deepest wounds come later in life. In the next chapter we will begin to expose the enemy of your soul who was behind many of your wounds.

Let's pray:

Holy and blessed Trinity. You know me. You are familiar with all my ways. Please help me. Revisiting the wounds of my past is so hard. I don't want to feel that pain again. Please come into those places in my heart that remain wounded and hold me there. Heal me there. And in your mercy, please reveal to me the vows I made; the ways I do not trust you. Forgive me and help me to grow in trusting you ever more truly. Please reveal to me more of who you are and who I am to you. In Jesus' name. Amen.

CHAPTER 5

A Special Hatred

All who hate me whisper about me,
imagining the worst for me.

—Psalm 41:7 NLT

In the companion book we began this chapter by telling the story of the cruel hailstorm that ravaged my once beautiful garden and left behind brokenness, debris, and sorrow. The destruction the storm caused felt like a mini passion play, a picture of the intentional assault against the daughters of Eve. This chapter asks us to reexamine our thoughts about the often brutal, nearly universal assault on femininity. Where does this come from?

Do not make the mistake of believing that "men are the enemy." Certainly men have had a hand in this and will have a day of reckoning before their Maker. But you will not understand this story—or your story— until you begin to see the actual Forces behind this assault and get a grip on their motives.

43

It is good to remember that God has not given us a spirit of fear, but of love, peace, and a sound mind. We do not need to fear the enemy. We have victory in Christ. But, we do need to expose his tactics and learn how to take a stand against them in the truth of God's Word.

FURTHER ASSAULT

If you will listen carefully to any woman's story, you will hear a theme: The assault on her heart. It might be obvious as in the stories of physical, verbal, or sexual abuse. Or it might be more subtle, the indifference of a world that cares nothing for her. Either way, the wounds continue to come long after we've "grown up," but they all seem to speak the same message. Our Question is answered again and again throughout our life, the message driven home into our hearts like a stake. Think of the story of your life. How has further assault come to you? Describe what you remember.

What messages were driven home into your heart?

Have you felt that you are essentially alone? If you do, do you believe it is because you are not the woman you should be?

Did you know that most women feel essentially alone?

WHAT IS REALLY GOING ON HERE?

The story of the treatment of women down through the ages is not a noble history. It has noble moments in it, to be sure, but taken as a whole, women have endured what seems to be a special hatred ever since we left Eden. What do you make of the degradation, the abuse, and the open assault that women around the world have endured? Are enduring even now?

Where does this hatred for women you see all over the world come from? Why is it so diabolical?

A SPECIAL HATRED

No explanation for the assault upon Eve and her daughters is sufficient unless it opens our eyes to the Prince of Darkness and his special hatred of femininity. (This is not to say that men [and women, for they, too, assault women] have no accountability in their treatment of women.) Have you ever wondered why Satan seems to make Eve the focus of his assault on humanity?

Satan was first named Lucifer, or Son of the Morning. It infers a glory, a brightness, a radiance unique to him. Look up Ezekiel 28:12–15. How does it describe Lucifer?

What happened? (See Ezekiel 28:17.)

Satan fell because of his beauty. Now his heart for revenge is to assault beauty.

BUT WHAT OF EVE?

She is the incarnation of the Beauty of God. More than anything else in all creation, she embodies the glory of God. She allures the world to God. Satan hates it with a jealousy we can only imagine.

And there is more. The Evil One also hates Eve because she gives life. Women nourish life. And they also bring life into the world soulfully, relationally, spiritually—in everything they touch.

Satan's bitter heart cannot bear it. He assaults her with a special hatred. History removes any doubt about this. It is even in the great stories—the villain goes after the Hero's true love, the Beauty. Can you think of some?

Satan's hatred of Eve and her daughters helps to explain an awful lot about your life's story. You are hated *because* of your beauty and power. Do you believe that could be possible?

Let your imagination go there for a little while. What would it feel like if it were true that you *are* beautiful, that you *are* powerful for the kingdom of God—and that is why you have endured the assault (and neglect) you have?

ON A HUMAN LEVEL

In this section, John was honest about his hesitancy to enter more fully into the world of women that writing *Captivating* with me would require. He also wrote about a deeper feeling that he sensed around women: A sense that was more like an allergic reaction to Back Off. Withdraw. Pull back. Pull away. Have you ever felt the men in your life get close only to withdraw, pull back? What happened? Who did you blame it on?

There is something diabolical at work here. Often when men do "back off" from their women, it is because they feel a strong pull to do so. Want to risk asking the man in your life if he has felt that? If you do ask him, then ask if he withdrew because he thought it was what you wanted him to do.

Back off, or *Leave her alone,* or *You don't really want to go there—she'll be too much for you* is something Satan has set against every woman from the day of her birth. And to every woman he has whispered, *You are alone, or When they see who you really are, you will be alone.* Quiet your heart and ask yourself, "Is this a message I have believed, feared, lived with?"

Not only do most women fear they will eventually be abandoned by the men in their lives—they fear it from other women as well. It's time to reveal this pervasive threat as the tool of the Enemy that it is. How long have you been living with a fear of abandonment? How much of your efforts to "be a good woman" or to make yourself beautiful are fueled by that fear?

THERE IS HOPE

The Evil One had a hand in all that has happened to you. If he didn't arrange for the assault directly—and certainly human sin has a large enough role to play—then he made sure he drove the message of the wounds home into your heart. He is the one who has dogged your heels with shame and self-doubt and accusation. He is the one who has done these things in order to prevent your restoration. For that is what he fears. He fears your beauty and your life-giving heart. What if it were true? How does that make you feel?

Now listen to the voice of your King. Read Isaiah 62:1–5. Who is Jerusalem?

What are you no longer called?

What are you called?

Read Jeremiah 30:16–17. How will God treat your enemies?

How will he treat you?

You really won't understand your life as a woman until you understand this: *You are passionately loved by the God of the universe. You are passionately hated by his Enemy.*

Dear heart, it is time for your restoration. For there is One greater than your Enemy. He has come to heal your broken heart and restore your feminine soul. Turn to him now:

Dear Jesus, I am beginning to see the assault on my life and on my heart, as coming from the enemy. He has been fierce against me. I have been wounded and wounded deeply. And I am trying to believe, beginning to believe, that it was not all my fault. Not what I deserved. Oh, God, please come to my battered heart and heal me. Come to the places in my heart where I have believed the enemy's lies to me for so long and speak the truth to me, there. In those places, I need you. I need your mercy. I need your covering, your kindness, and your touch. Make me quick to recognize the ploys of the enemy and teach me to stand against them. Please come for me, Jesus. And heal me. In your name, I pray. Amen.

CHAPTER 6

Healing the Wound

I didn't know just what was wrong with me,
Till your love helped me name it.

—ARETHA FRANKLIN

Jesus said, don't you think God cares just a little bit more for you than for the birds of the air? "Are you not much more valuable than they?" (Matt. 6:26). Indeed, you are. You, dear heart, are the crown of his creation, his glorious image bearer. And he will do everything it takes to rescue you, and set your heart free.

We all need Jesus to come for us. And we never stop needing him to come, to touch, to heal, and to restore our hearts. The journey of becoming ever more healed, ever more his, is such an important one, we think it would be good to take the time your heart needs and walk through this chapter slowly, carefully, with God tenderly holding your heart.

What in your heart do you really want him to heal, touch, and restore? Ask him to help you.

THE OFFER

What have you been taught is the primary reason that Jesus came to earth?

Jesus proclaims his mission when he takes the scroll of Isaiah and begins his public ministry. (See Isaiah 61:1–3.) This scripture must be important to him. It must be central. . . . Let me try and state it here.

God has sent me on a mission.
I have some great news for you.
God has sent me to restore and release something.
And that something is you.
I am here to give you back your heart and set you free.
I am furious at the Enemy who did this to you, and I will fight against him.
Let me comfort you.
For, dear one, I will bestow beauty upon you
where you have known only devastation.
Joy, in the places of your deep sorrow.
And I will robe your heart in thankful praise
in exchange for your resignation and despair.

Now that is an offer worth considering. What if it were true? What if Jesus could and would do this for your broken heart, your wounded feminine soul?

He can, and he will. If you'll let him. The Son of God has come to ransom you, and to heal your broken, wounded, bleeding heart and to set you free from bondage. He came to restore the glorious creation that you are. And then to set you free—to be yourself.

HEMMED IN

Why did God curse Eve with loneliness and heartache, an emptiness that nothing would be able to fill? . . . He did it to *save* her. For as we all know personally, something in Eve's heart shifted at the Fall. Something sent its roots down deep into her soul—and ours—that mistrust of God's heart, that resolution to find life on our own terms. So God has to thwart her. In love, he has to block her attempts until, wounded and aching, she turns to him and him alone for her rescue.

Jesus has to thwart us, too—thwart our self-redemptive plans, our controlling and our hiding, and thwart the ways we are seeking to fill the ache within us. Otherwise, we would never fully turn to him for our rescue. . . . And so you will see the gentle, firm hand of God in a woman's life hemming her in. What *hasn't* been going well in your life for some time? How is God thwarting you?

Listen carefully: Not every distress in our life is brought by our God. We don't believe even most of them are. We have an enemy who comes to steal, kill, and destroy. Ask God to show you where he has been thwarting you. Life apart from God will not work. He is thwarting you because he loves you.

TURNING FROM THE WAYS YOU'VE SOUGHT TO SAVE YOURSELF

We construct a life of safety ("I will not be vulnerable there") and find some place to get a taste of being enjoyed, or at least, of being "needed." Our journey toward healing beings when we repent of those ways, lay them down, let them go.

Like the Prodigal we wake one day to see that the life we've constructed is no life at all. We let desire speak to us again; we let our hearts have a voice, and what the voice usually says is, this isn't working. My life is a disaster. Jesus—I'm sorry. Forgive me. Please come for me. Are you ready and willing to say this to Jesus? Be specific—what do you need to lay down? Repent of? Let go?

INVITE HIM IN

There is a famous passage of Scripture that many people have heard in the context of an invitation to know Christ as Savior. "Behold, I stand at the door and knock. If anyone hears My voice and opens the door, I will come in" (Rev. 3:20 NKJV). It might come as a surprise that Christ asks our permission to come in and heal, but he is kind, and the door is shut from the inside, and healing never comes against our will. He knocks through our loneliness. He knocks through our sorrows. He knocks through many things, waiting for us to give him permission to enter in. What is God "knocking" through these days? How is God stirring your heart?

Give him permission to enter. Give him access to your broken heart. Sit quietly. Wait. Journal your thoughts, feelings, desires.

RENOUNCE THE AGREEMENTS YOU'VE MADE

Your wounds brought messages with them. They had a similar theme. Because they were delivered with such pain, they *felt* true. What "messages" have dogged you all these years? What did you come to believe about yourself? Write them down.

Before we are entirely convinced that they aren't true, we must reject the message of our wounds. It's a way of unlocking the door to Jesus. Agreements lock the door from the inside. Renouncing the agreements unlocks the door to him. Jump in. If you feel ready or not, let Jesus in.

WE FIND OUR TEARS

Part of the reason women are so tired is because we are spending so much energy trying to "keep it together." We want to give you permission to fall apart. To be a mess. Does that thought frighten you? Why?

Let the tears come. It is the only kind thing to do for your woundedness. Allow yourself to feel again. And feel you will—many things. Let it all out.

FORGIVE

Okay—now for a hard step (as if the others have been easy). A real step of courage and will. We must forgive those who hurt us. Again. Paul warns us that unforgiveness and bitterness can wreck our lives and the lives of others (Eph. 4:31; Heb. 12:15). We have to let it all go. Who do you still hold in your heart in anger, resentment, unforgiveness? Be honest.

Forgiveness is a choice. It is not a feeling—don't try and feel forgiving. It is an act of the will. We acknowledge that it hurt, that it mattered, and we choose to extend forgiveness to our fathers, our mothers, those who hurt us. This is not saying, "It didn't really matter"; it is not saying, "I probably deserved part of it anyway." Forgiveness says, "It was wrong. Very wrong. It mattered, hurt me deeply. And I release you. I give you to God."

It might help to remember that those who hurt you were also deeply wounded themselves. Can you see that in them, in their life stories?

Pray now. Release them to God. Who are they? What are you forgiving them for?

ASK JESUS TO HEAL YOU

Healing is available. This is the offer of our Savior—to heal our broken hearts. To come to the young places within us and find us there, take us in his arms, bring us home. The time has come to let Jesus heal you. Pray. Sit quietly. And rest assured that Jesus has heard your cry, has come for you, and will continue to come. Listen for his voice. What is he saying to you?

ASK HIM TO DESTROY YOUR ENEMIES

There are things you've struggled with all your life. You probably thought that those were just your fault. But they are not. They came from the Enemy who wanted to take your heart captive. What enemies of your soul would you like Jesus to destroy? Self-contempt? A spirit of overwhelmed? Fear? Shame?

LET HIM FATHER YOU

There is a part of our hearts that was made for Daddy, made for his strong and tender love. That part is still there, and longing. Open it to Jesus, and to your Father God. Ask him to come and love you there.

ASK HIM TO ANSWER YOUR QUESTION

You still have a Question, dear one. We all do. We all still need to know, *Do you see me? Am I captivating? Do I have a beauty all my own?*

Let's just start with a thought. What if the message delivered with your wounds simply isn't true about you? Let that sink in. Ponder that. It wasn't true. What does it free you to do? Weep? Rejoice? Let go? Take your heart back?

Now take your questions to Jesus. Ask him to show you your beauty.

Dear Jesus, I am almost afraid to ask, but I so need the answer. I need the questions of my deepest heart answered. And answered truthfully. Answered by you. Lord, how do you see me? As a woman. Am I captivating to you? Am I lovely? Would you please show me my beauty? Show me what you think of me. I want to hear from you. Open the eyes of my heart that I may recognize and receive your answers as you bring them to me. I need to know, God. I will wait and listen. For I love you, and my heart is yours. All this I pray, in the name of Jesus. Amen.

CHAPTER 7

Romanced

Romance is the deepest thing in life.
It is deeper even than reality.

—G. K. CHESTERTON

The truth that what God—the Ageless Romancer—wants most from us is our hearts' love; that he is captivated by *us* is almost too marvelous for words. He sees something in us that we don't yet see. It is hard to grasp that we are extravagantly loved by the God of the Universe. But it is *true*. Having our hearts begin to grasp the depth of Jesus' personal, intimate, intentional love for us, changes us. In all the best ways.

We need his help here. We need revelation from him about his love of us.

LONGING FOR ROMANCE

As women we long to be loved in a certain way, a way unique to our femininity. We long for romance. We are wired for it; it's what makes our hearts come alive. You know that. But what you might never have known is this. *Romance doesn't need to wait for a man.* God longs to bring this into your life himself.

God wants to heal us through his love to become mature women who actually know him. He wants us to experience verses like, "Therefore I am

59

now going to allure her; I will lead her into the desert and speak tenderly to her" (Hos. 2:14).

Dream a little. What would it be like to experience for yourself that the truest thing about God's heart toward yours is not disappointment or disapproval but *deep, fiery, passionate love*? What would change in your life?

What would change in the way you perceive God?

Faithful obedience to God is vital, but it is not all God draws us to. It is not sufficient for our healing. What do we need to live the life God has called us to—or better, *invited* us to live?

In this chapter I said, "The root of all holiness is Romance." When you love someone, you want to please them. You do want to do the things they want to do. The same holds true in your walk with God. Does that begin to make sense to you—that romance with God is the root of all holiness?

GOD AS LOVER

Think about the movies that you love. Think of one of the most romantic scenes you can remember, scenes that make you sigh. What are they?

Now put yourself in the scene as the Beauty and Jesus as the Lover. What does your heart do with that?

It's okay. It's quite biblical. Jesus calls himself the Bridegroom (Matt. 9:15; 25:1–10; John 3:29). Now, you'll need to take the religious drapery and sanctimonious gilding off of this. "Bridegroom" simply means fiancé. Lover. This is the most intimate of all the metaphors Jesus chose to describe his love and longing for us, and the kind of relationship he invites us into.

The Great Love Story the Scriptures are telling us about also reveals a Lover who longs for you. *The story of your life is also the story of the long and passionate pursuit of your heart by the One who knows you best and loves you most.*

God has written the Romance not only on our hearts but all over the world around us. What we need is for him to open our eyes, to open our ears that we might recognize his voice calling to us, see his hand wooing us in the beauty that quickens our hearts.

What are some of your favorite memories?

What were the things that romanced your heart as a girl? Was it horses in a field? Was it the fragrance of the air after a summer rain?

Those were all whispers from your Lover, notes to awaken your heart's longings. And as we as women journey into a true intimacy with God, he often brings those things back into our lives, to remind us he was there, to heal and restore things that were lost or stolen. What would you like God to restore to you?

OPENING OUR HEARTS TO THE ROMANCER

Every song you love, every memory you cherish, every moment that has moved you to holy tears has been given to you from the One who has been pursuing you from your first breath in order to win your heart. Ask God for the eyes to see how he is romancing your heart today. What are the things that take your breath away? The things that make you cry or fill your heart with longing?

The romancing of your heart will be immensely personal. God knows what moves you. Ask him to romance you this week, even today.

THE EBB AND FLOW

This is not to say that our lives are lived as one big romantic moment with Jesus It is saying, however, that the Romance is the foundation of our relationship with him. How would you describe your relationship with God over the past several months?

The ebbing in our experience of God is to draw out our hearts in deeper longing. In the times of emptiness, an open heart notices. When you are aware of an ebbing in your heart with God, what do you feel?

How do you usually handle your heart when it is aching?

What is crucial is that next time, we handle our hearts differently. We ask our Lover to come for us, and we keep our hearts open to his coming. And he comes, dear hearts. He does come. The times of intimacy—the flowing waters of love—those times then bring healing to places in our hearts that still need his touch. Where are the places you would like him to come? To heal? To love?

Ask him to come.

WHAT DOES GOD WANT FROM YOU?

Over the years what have you believed God most wanted from you? Was it obedience? Trust? What?

Are you beginning to grasp more deeply what it is that God wants from you? What he is after?

You've probably heard that there is in every human heart a place that God alone can fill. But there is also in God's heart a place that you alone can fill. You are the one who takes his breath away by your beautiful heart that, against all odds, hopes in him. Let it be true of you. Sit with that truth. Ponder it. What is your heart's response?

In order to have intimacy with you, he has gone to great lengths . . . and continues to do so. Here's how the flow goes in Hosea.

> Therefore I will block her path with thornbushes;
> I will wall her in so that she cannot find her way.
> She will chase after her lovers but not catch them;
> she will look for them but not find them.
> —Hosea 2:6–7 NKJV

> "In that day," declares the LORD,
> "you will call me 'my husband';
> you will no longer call me 'my master.'

> "I will betroth you to me forever;
> I will betroth you in righteousness and justice,
> in love and compassion."
> —Hosea 2:16, 19

You may have questions here for God. Go ahead and ask him.

ADORING HEARTS

An intimate relationship with Jesus is for each and every one of us. God wants intimacy with you. In order to have it, you, too, must offer it to him.

65

As Jesus and his disciples were on their way, he came to a village where a woman named Martha opened her home to him. She had a sister called Mary, who was at the Lord's feet listening to what he said. But Martha was distracted by all the preparations that had to be made. She came to him and asked, "Lord, don't you care that my sister has left me to do the work by myself? Tell her to help me!"

"Martha, Martha," the Lord answered, "you are worried and upset about many things, but only one thing is needed. Mary has chosen what is better, and it will not be taken away from her."

—Luke 10:38–42

Mary recognized who Jesus was—the Source of all Life. Love Incarnate. She dropped everything and sat at his feet, fixing the gaze of her heart upon him. Take a few minutes and turn your heart toward Jesus. Tell him why he is worthy of your love.

Martha is a picture of the distracted bride. There is so much to be done. What is distracting you? Make a list.

A woman's worship brings Jesus immense pleasure and a deep ministry. You can minister to the heart of God. How does that make you feel?

God is waiting. He longs for you. Offer your heart to him.

CULTIVATING INTIMACY

Intimacy with Jesus takes cultivating. To become intentional about cultivating a heart of worship, a heart of devoted adoration is a beautiful thing. Do you want this? If so, what will you have to let go of in order to make room for private worship in your life?

To pursue intimacy with Christ, you will have to fight for it. You'll need to fight busyness. You'll need to fight the Thief that would steal your Lover's gifts to you outright. That's okay. There is a fierceness in women that was given to us for a purpose. What will *you* have to fight?

Ask his help in making you desperately hungry for him. Ask his help in creating the time and space you need to draw close to him. Ask him to reveal himself to you as the Lover that he is. Get in a private place. Bring your Bible and a journal to write down what you hear God say in the depths of your heart. Ask the Holy Spirit to come and help you worship Jesus. Find time this week to give it a try. Give yourself at least half an hour.

To be spiritual is to be in a Romance with God. What is your heart's response now to that truth?

Jesus is better than you thought! And as we grow in knowing him, he just continues to get more so. Come. Sit at his feet.

> One thing I ask of the Lord,
> this is what I seek;
> that I may dwell in the house of the Lord
> all the days of my life,
> to gaze upon the beauty of the Lord
> and to seek him in his temple.
> —Psalm 27:4

CHAPTER 8

Beauty to Unveil

Show me your face, let me hear your voice;
for your voice is sweet, and your face is lovely.

—SONG OF SONGS 2:14 NKJV

This chapter is devoted to beginning to unveil what beauty is and its redemptive, life-giving place in our world. And you possess it, simply by being a woman. *For beauty is the essence of femininity.*

Before we journey further, pray and ask Jesus to come, help you.

THE STRENGTH OF A MAN

The essence of a man is Strength. A man is meant to be the incarnation—our experience in human form—of our Warrior God. A God who comes through for us. Isn't that what we, as women, long to experience from our man, and from the men in our lives? How have you experienced masculine strength in good ways, personally?

Have you ever had a man step in spiritually on your behalf? How?

Have you ever had a man step in physically on your behalf? How?

Do you understand that by strength we don't mean big muscles? So then you can see that when we speak about the essence of a woman—her beauty—we don't mean "the perfect figure." The beauty of a woman is first a soulish beauty.

THE ESSENCE OF A WOMAN

The essence of a woman is Beauty. She is meant to be the incarnation— our experience in human form—of a Captivating God. *A God who invites us.* Beauty is what the world longs to experience from a woman. So listen to this: beauty is an essence that dwells in every woman. It was given to her by God. It was given to you. Do you believe that?

What is beautiful to you?
   In art?

In nature?

In others?

All beauty speaks of God. For God is nothing if not Beautiful. Simone Weil wrote, "The soul's inclination to love beauty is the trap God most frequently uses in order to win it."

Beauty is core to a woman—who she is and what she longs to be—and one of the most glorious ways we bear the image of God in a broken and often ugly world. How do you bring beauty to your world?

How do you long to?

BEAUTY FLOWS FROM A HEART AT REST

Beauty is the most essential and, yes, the most misunderstood of all the feminine qualities. The only things standing in the way of our beauty are our doubts and fears and the hiding and striving we fall to as a result. Think of a friend whom you find truly lovely. What is it about her that is so lovely?

Who is qualified to speak to your heart of the beauty found there? God. Keep asking him.

A woman is most beautiful when she is at rest. The choice a woman makes is not to conjure beauty but to let her defenses down and just let her heart show up. Beauty comes with it. What do you think of that?

Have you seen it? The true loveliness that shines out of a woman when she is freely enjoying herself?

> Your beauty should not come from outward adornment, such as braided hair and the wearing of gold jewelry and fine clothes. Instead, it should be that of your inner self, the unfading beauty of a gentle and quiet spirit.
>
> —1 Peter 3:3–4

How have you understood this scripture?

First, Peter is trying to say that true beauty comes from the inner part of us: our hearts. A heart at rest. To have a gentle and quiet spirit is to have *a heart of faith*; a heart that trusts in God, a spirit that has been quieted by his love and filled with his peace, not a heart that is striving and restless.

A woman in her glory, a woman of beauty, knows in her quiet center where God dwells that he finds her beautiful, has deemed her worthy, and in him, she is enough. Ask him what he thinks of you as a woman. His words to you let you rest and unveil your beauty. Wait for his answer. When it comes, write it down. Hold on to it.

The hardest part of asking God what he sees in you as a woman, asking him to answer your deepest questions about your beauty is this: believing what he says. Because he will speak, dear friends, and what he will say will be so very close to what your heart has wanted to hear all these years. Accept what he has to say.

Beauty Is Inviting

Beauty beckons us. Beauty invites us. Come; explore; immerse yourself. God—Beauty himself—invites us to know him. He wants to be known, to be explored. And a woman does too. Have you ever had the experience of wanting to get closer to something beautiful? Maybe even become a part of it?

The way we choose to live is the way we invite others to live. A woman who is striving invites others to strive. What's it like to be around a striving woman? What do you feel the pressure to do? And, what *don't* you feel free to do?

By contrast, a woman whose heart is at rest invites others to rest too. What's it like to be around a restful woman? What do you feel the freedom to do?

What are *you* most often inviting others to do? Do you have the courage to ask them?

What do you *want* to invite others to?

A woman whose heart has been quieted by the Love of God, invites others to LIFE when she unveils her beauty. Redeemed Eve is the incarnation of the heart of God for intimacy. She says to the world, . . . you are wanted here. Come in. Share yourself. Be enjoyed. Enjoy me as I share myself. As you begin to live like this, you discover the places in your heart that still need the healing touch of Jesus. Jesus invites us to live as an inviting woman now and to find our healing along the way. What is your heart's response to this?

OFFERING BEAUTY

For a woman to unveil her beauty means she is offering her heart. Not primarily her works or her usefulness (think Martha in the kitchen), but offering her presence. What does that mean to you?

Have you sat with a friend and had their undivided attention and interest? Have you had others ask you, "How are you doing?" and really want to know . . . and they're willing to wait for your answer? How did that feel?

That is offering the gift of *presence* . . . being present in every way, physically, emotionally, mentally. It means listening to someone wholeheartedly, engaged, without thinking of what you have to do next or what you will say next. That is what we need from others. And that is what others need from us. When we offer our unguarded presence, we live like Jesus. And we invite others to do the same.

Beauty offers mercy. A kind word. A gentle response. Do you struggle with offering mercy, kindness, and patience to anyone? Who?

Ask God to help you offer mercy, light, laughter, kindness. Pay attention to how it goes. Beauty isn't demanding. It speaks from desire. To offer your heart is to offer your *desire,* instead of your demand.

OF COURSE IT FEELS RISKY

The scariest thing for a man is to offer his strength in situations where he doesn't know if it will make any difference. Or worse, that he will fail. If he fears intimacy, then offering strength means offering intimacy. If he fears failing in his career, offering his strength means taking a promotion or accepting a new and risky project. Have you seen that played out?

In the same way, the scariest thing for women is to offer our beauty into situations where we don't know if it will make any difference. Or worse, that we will be rejected. . . . We, too, must take risks. What is the scariest thing for you to offer? When?

If you are married, imagine that your husband comes home with a serious expression on his face and asks you to come, sit down, he wants to talk with you privately. What would you feel? What would you want to do?

Peter gives us what might be the secret to releasing a woman's heart and her beauty: "Do not give way to fear" (1 Peter 3:6). Isn't that why we hide, why we strive, why we control, why we do anything but offer beauty? We have given way to fear. Have you asked yourself how much you are motivated by fear? Ask yourself now, how much?

God invites us, urges us to repent of our self-protective strategies. And to rest in his love for us, to not give way to fear, but to trust him.

We can't wait until we feel safe to love and invite. In fact, if you feel a little scared, then you're probably on the right path. What is God calling you to risk?

What will it require from you? More faith in him? More healing of your heart? Sounds like the right track.

Sadly, there will be times when our offer of our true hearts is not received well. Jesus offered like no other, and many rejected him. When that happens to us, God's invitation to us is to bring our sorrow to him to keep our hearts open and alive and to find our heart's refuge and healing in his love.

LETTING OUR HEARTS BE DEEPENED

To possess true beauty, we must be willing to suffer. I don't like that. Just writing it down makes my heart shrink back. Yet, if Christ himself was perfected through his sufferings, why would I believe God would not do the same with me? With you?

God does not always rescue us out of a painful season. You know that he does not always give to us what we so desperately want when we want it. He is after something much more valuable than our happiness. He is restoring and growing in us an eternal weight of glory. And sometimes it hurts. What was a recent (or is a current) very difficult season for you? What was/is happening?

What went on (or is going on) in your relationship with God? In your faith?

A heart awakened to its sorrow is more aware, more present, more alive. To all of the facets of life.

CULTIVATING BEAUTY

Life is harsh on a woman's heart. The assault on our beauty is real. But Jesus is urging us now to care for ourselves, watch over our hearts (Prov. 4:23). The world needs your beauty. That is why you are here. Your heart and your beauty are something to be treasured and nourished. What are some ways you can nourish your heart?

Where do you feel closest to God?

If you had a whole day that you could do anything you wanted, what would the day look like? Where would you be? Would you be alone or with someone? Dream a little.

We need to listen to the voice of God in our hearts as he tells us what we need and then go do that! He knows what would be best for us. Often what he will tell us we need to do is something that we really enjoy. Ask him if he would like to make your dream day happen. Ask him for it. (Or to happen really close to what your dream is.)

The Holy Spirit is our guide, our counselor, our comforter, our Great Friend, and he will lead us. Abiding in Christ means attending to the voice of God within, nourishing our own hearts and nourishing our relationship with him. Over time.

And guess what! Contrary to what the world claims, Beauty does not diminish with time; Beauty deepens and increases. *True beauty comes from a depth of soul that can only be attained through living many years well.* God grows it in us.

As we gaze on Jesus, as we behold his goodness, and his glory, we are changed into his likeness, the most beautiful Person of all. What is your response to that?

When a woman knows that she is loved and loved deeply, she has had her heart's deepest questions answered: "Am I lovely? Am I worth fighting for? Have I been and will I continue to be romanced?" When these questions are answered, "Yes," a restful, quiet spirit settles in a woman's heart. *And every woman can have these questions answered, "Yes."*

When we are at rest in the knowledge that our God *really* loves us, we can offer our hearts to others and invite them to Life.

FAITH, HOPE, AND LOVE

Unveiling our beauty really just means unveiling our feminine hearts. It's scary, for sure. That is why it is our greatest expression of faith, hope, and love. How will offering and unveiling your heart require you to live by faith?

How will it require you to hope in God?

How will it cause you to love others sincerely?

When we offer our Beauty, we are living a life of love so that others' hearts might come alive, be healed, and grow in knowing God. And that is a noble, worthy life to live.

Take a few moments now and express your heart's desire to God.

CHAPTER 9

Arousing Adam

Are you strong enough to be my man?

—SHERYL CROW

When it comes to the subject of loving a man—any of the men in your life—we need far more than a chapter. The issues are often murky, and things can get really muddy as times goes by. But we cannot pass over this subject, either. Too many questions linger here for most women. So we will try and lay out in this chapter the deeper issues and trust the Holy Spirit to help you with the application.

Everything we said about unveiling beauty, about how a woman invites and offers—this is so much more true when it comes to loving Adam. *True femininity calls forth true masculinity.* Let's ask Jesus to help us go deeper into understanding men and how best to call forth their true masculinity.

ADAM'S WOUND

If you'll watch little boys for any length of time, you'll see how deeply the Hero is written on their hearts. Their games are filled with battle and courage and testing. What crazy things have your sons, your brothers, your girlfriend's sons done to test themselves?

When boys become teenagers, they take on an air of independence and bravado that can really drive moms nuts. It looks arrogant and defiant, but what it really is is their masculine strength emerging in an awkward stage. In all of this, can you see their Question: *Do I have what it takes? Am I the real deal? Am I a man?*

A man's deepest wounds come from the way his Question was answered in his youth. Just like yours. Every man is wounded. As he was growing up, he looked to his father to answer his Question. The result was often devastating. In the case of violent fathers, the wound is given directly. In the case of passive fathers, the wound is given indirectly.

Adam's sin and Adam's woundedness come together to result in the passivity or the drivenness you find in so many men. You won't begin to understand a man until you understand his Question, his wound, and how Adam also fell. His search for validation is the driving force of his life. Think of the men you are closest to. How do you think their Question was answered?

Can *you* answer it? As much as you'd like to, you can only speak to it. You can't answer a man's deepest question. Only masculinity can bestow masculinity.

STANDING IN LOVE'S WAY

In *Wild at Heart* I warned men that the greatest obstacle to loving a woman was this: too many men take their Question to Eve. They look to her for the validation of their souls. Haven't you felt it?

It happens usually around adolescence, this fatal shift. The father has been silent or violent; his chance to redeem his son is nearly gone. The next window that opens in a boy's journey is his sexuality. Suddenly, he is aware of Eve. She looks like life itself to him. She looks like the answer to his Question.

So much of the pornography addiction for men comes from this. It's not about sex—it's about validation. She makes him feel like a man. She offers him her beauty, and it makes him feel strong. Pornography is about a man trying to get his masculinity validated in a way that requires nothing of him. How do you respond to reading this?

A woman can be a man's *ezer*, his companion, his inspiration. But she cannot be the validation of his soul. Men have got to take their Question to their Father in heaven. Only he knows who we truly are. A man goes to Eve to offer his strength.

Now, the same holds true for you, Eve. You cannot take your Question to Adam. You cannot look to him for the validation of your soul. In what ways are you looking to Adam to answer your heart's Question?

Ask Jesus to show you what you've been doing with your Question and how you've related to Adam. Only then can we talk about loving men.

HOW DOES A WOMAN LOVE A MAN?

Let's start with sex. *Not* because "it's all men think about" (as many a cynical woman has said), but because it presents the relationship between femininity and masculinity in such a clear way. It is a very passionate and heightened picture for a much broader reality. The question before us is, "How does a woman best love a man?" The answer is simple: Seduce him. What do you think of this answer?

The beauty of a woman is what arouses the strength of a man. He *wants* to play the man when a woman acts like that. He *wants* to come through. And this is crucial—don't you want him to *want* to?

Switch positions. Who would you rather spend an evening with, the man that says, "You look beautiful tonight!" or "You're going out in *that?*" Which man generates a desire to become ever more beautiful?

Think beyond the bedroom. What are some ways that a good woman could seduce a good man? How could you, as a woman, arouse desire in a man to exert his masculine strength in good ways? *To grow into becoming a more godly man?*

Inviting strength, alluring strength is much more effective than demanding strength, challenging strength. There are times when we need to evoke from our men movement; we need to call forth their masculinity. How do we *best* do that?

THE HOLY, SCANDALOUS WOMEN OF THE BIBLE

There are five women mentioned in the genealogy of Jesus. Now, that might not strike you as a big deal, until you understand that women are never mentioned in those genealogies. It's *always* men. These are really good women.

What distinguishes these women? What can we learn from them? How did they live in ways that called forth strength in the men in their lives? The common theme is this. *Courage, Cunning,* and *Stunning Vulnerability.*

Go back to the book and reread the section about Ruth. John wrote, "She can badger him: *All you do is work, work, work. Why won't you stand up and be a man?* She can whine about it: *Boaz, pleeease hurry up and marry me.* She can emasculate him: *I thought you were a real man; I guess I was wrong.* Or she can use all she is as a woman to get him to use all he's got as a man. She can arouse, inspire, energize—seduce him."

Which kind of approach would you say you tend to take with the man/men in your life?

Which kind of approach do you believe will best achieve the desired results?

Ruth *aroused* Boaz to play the man. *She awakened his desire to be the Hero.*

EMASCULATING WOMEN

Women pretty much fall into one of three categories: Dominating Women, Desolate Women, or Arousing Women. The first two are what happens to Eve as a result of the Fall. The third is a woman whose femininity is being restored by God and who offers it to others. How would you describe yourself?

When a woman becomes controlling and not in the least vulnerable, her seductivity is shut down. The message is "Back off—I'll handle this." Any wonder that he backs off?

So many women fear the wildness God put in their man. They are drawn to his strength and then set about taming him once they've "caught" him. Have you seen that done? Have you done it? What was the effect on the man?

Emasculating women send a clear message: "I don't need you. I refuse to be vulnerable and inviting. You have nothing to offer me." How can you let your man know you need him? How can you be more vulnerable and inviting?

Okay. Here's a piece of daring advice. Have him read this chapter and then ask him what kind of woman you've been like to live with. I know—it sounds absolutely crazy. Too risky. But it just might open up whole new levels of intimacy, too!

Desolate Women

Desolate women don't seem at first pass to be all that emasculating. They don't attack or dominate. But neither do they allure. A man in her presence feels uninvited. Unwanted. It's a form of rejection, emasculation, to be sure. But it's harder to point out because it's so subtle. Have you been like this toward your man, or men in general? Why?

Desolate women can also be those whose ache is what *defines* them. Women who will do whatever it takes to get a man. The Woman at the Well would be an example. She moves from lover to lover trying to fill the void within her. She's available—but in a clingy, desperate way. Men use women like this—but they do not love them. They do not feel challenged to be a Hero. Desolate women do not call the men in their lives to be

Heroes. Have you been like this—desperate for a man to love you, so desperate you have thrown yourself at him, been *too* vulnerable? How did it go?

AROUSING WOMEN

Okay. We are on the road to redemption; we are in the process of being restored. We are becoming the women we want to be, but we know we have often lived like Eve after the Fall. If you have been either a dominating and controlling woman, or a desolate and mousy woman— what would repentance look like for you? How can you begin to change the way you relate to your man?

How about sexually?

How about relationally, in the way you speak and relate to one another?

How about with decisions such as finances?

Arousing women are those who call forth the best in a man by offering who they are *as* a woman. Women who offer beauty, their true heart. How can you begin to communicate this to your man: "You are an amazing man"?

A man needs to hear from his woman more than anything else: *I need you. I need your strength. I believe in you. You have what it takes.* What can you do to "say" this to your man?

Granted, not every man is on the road to redemption. There are men out there who are not safe and good men. Some of you are married to one. All of you will encounter them. How do you love them? With great wisdom and cunning. A woman can test to see if a man is willing to move in a good direction by offering a *taste* of what is available with her if he does. She does not give everything in a moment. Like God does, she allures, and waits to see what he will do.

If you are in a difficult marriage, we strongly urge you to get some outside perspective. If you think you might be in an abusive situation—if your man abuses you verbally or physically or sexually—we STRONGLY urge you to see a counselor. Do not think "things will get better." Not without help, they won't.

SINGLE WOMEN

Mary, Rahab, Ruth, and Tamar were all single women when the story of their greatness was told. They are such powerful reminders that this can be lived out as a single woman. They also stand in stark contrast to some of the messages of "purity" given single women today. To our single readers— what have you been taught a godly approach to young men looks like?

A woman should be alluring to the man she is attracted to. A smile, a tenderness, an interest in him and his life are natural and welcome. Yes, you can offer beauty to him—in gently increasing amounts, as he pursues and comes closer. And yes, there are parts of you that should be held as mysteries until he fully commits, and you offer yourself to him on your wedding night. Don't offer everything, but don't offer nothing. On a scale of 1 to10, with 1 being nothing and 10 being sleeping with a man you are not married to in order to "catch him," where would you put yourself? And why?

How much, and when? Walk with God. Be a wise and discerning woman. Invite, arouse, and maintain your personal integrity.

You've traveled some ways in this journal and looked at your wounds and the assaults you've endured, and seen some of the ways they have shaped you into the woman you are now. Can you see the way your past is shaping the way you relate to men?

Be careful you do not offer too much of yourself to a man until you have good, solid evidence that he is a strong man willing to commit. Look at his track record with other women. Does he have any close male friends— what are *they* like as men? Can he hold down a job? Is he walking with God in a real and intimate way? How does the man in your life measure up?

Woman was given to man to be his *ezer*—his *lifesaver*. It's a challenging job and can only be done well by a woman who is in an intimate, holy Romance with God. He will guide us. He will teach us. God allures us to himself. He invites us to join him in alluring others to him as well.

Arousing Adam means alluring the men in your life to God. Not by demanding. Not by controlling. But by faith, hope, and love enticing them to become ever more the man God created them to be.

And how exactly do we do that? By first becoming ever more the woman God created us to be. What would that look like in your life today?

Let's pray.

Dear Jesus. I don't quite understand this yet. I know the adage that you catch more bees with honey than with vinegar, but how do I entice men to godliness without manipulating them? You say in your Word that a godly woman can win her unbelieving husband to Christ by her behavior. I want to become a woman who entices the men in my life to become more yours through my behavior, my life-giving words, and my feminine heart. Teach me, Lord. In Jesus' name. Amen.

CHAPTER 10

Mothers, Daughters, Sisters

Adam named his wife Eve, because she would
become the mother of all the living.

—Genesis 3:20

We have mother earth from which all growing things come and Mother Nature, the unpredictable source of typhoons and tornadoes. The mother lode is the source of riches, and a "mother headache" is one that sends you to bed. The mother of all storms is fierce, and the motherland is the home we left and long for. Mother is the source of life. Mother is powerful. Mother is strong. Mother can nurture, and mother can destroy. Depending on our individual experiences, the word *mother* can evoke images of a warm, welcoming woman or turn our blood to ice.

Whether good or bad, whether redemptive or destructive, our relationships with our mothers affected us to the core of our beings, helping to shape us into the women we have become. This chapter is devoted to the holy, rocky terrain of relationships among and between women. Before we journey deeper into this realm, let's ask for God's hand to hold our hearts and guide us.

OUR MOTHERS

We are not all mothers, but we all had one. Or longed for one. The relationship between a mother and daughter is a holy, tender, fierce thing fraught with land mines and umbilical cords that stretch and sometimes strangle. Put a few words to what your relationship with your mother was like when you were young. What do you remember? Any special moments? Any painful memories?

Did your relationship with your mother change when you became an adolescent? What was it like?

Did she know the deeper waters of your heart?

You have probably heard it said that you cannot pass on what you do not possess. It means that a woman with very low self-esteem will be unable to pass on very high self-esteem to her daughter, even though she may want to very much. We received from our mothers some of the same issues that they struggled deeply with even though they may play out differently in our lives. Unintentionally, our brokenness gets passed down. What is your relationship with your mom like these days? Would you say you are close?

Many a good woman makes the desperate mistake of believing that her daughter is a reflection of herself, an extension of herself, and therefore the verdict on her as a mother, and as a woman. Did your mother feel this way about you?

Girls' hearts flourish in homes where they are seen and invited to become ever more themselves. Parents who enjoy their daughters are giving them and the world a great gift. Mothers in particular have the opportunity to offer encouragement to their daughters by inviting them into their feminine world and by treasuring their daughter's unique beauty.

THE LONG ROAD HOME

Is your mother someone that you have a relationship with, or would like to?

How do you feel around your mother?

How do you think she feels around you?

What would the best possible relationship with your mother look like? Put some words to your heart's desire. Dream big.

Now, go ahead, and ask God for it.

THE COST

It is one thing to suffer. It is something far worse to walk alongside one you love who is suffering intensely and be unable to do anything about it. Many of you have lived this. You know. Have you experienced this? With whom? What was happening?

A woman bleeds when she gives birth, but that is only the beginning of the bleeding. A heart enlarged by all a mother endures with and through her child's life, all a mother prays and works and hopes for on her child's behalf, bleeds too. If you have children, what are you aching for in their lives?

TO MOTHER

As large as the role is that our mothers have played, the word *mother* is more powerful when used as a verb than as a noun. All women are not mothers, but all women are called to mother. To mother is to nurture, to train, to educate, to rear. In doing this, women partner with Christ in the vital mission of bringing forth life. Who has mothered you in the course of your life? How?

Who have you mothered? How?

All women are called to mother. And all women are called to give birth. Women give birth to all kinds of things—to a book, to a church, or to a movement. Women give birth to ideas, to creative expressions, to ministries. We birth life in others by inviting them into deeper realms of healing, to deeper walks with God, to deeper intimacy with Jesus. A woman is not less of a woman because she is not a wife or has not physically borne a child. The heart and life of a woman are much more vast than that. What have you "given birth" to?

What would you love to give birth to?

MY SISTER, MY FRIEND

All women are made in the image of God in that we bring forth life. When we enter into our world and into the lives of those we love and offer our tender and strong feminine hearts, we cannot help but mother them. I love the way women friends have with each other. When I gather with a group of women friends, inevitably someone begins to rub someone else's back. Merciful, tender, caressing, healing touches are given. Have you seen this? Experienced it?

The capacity of a woman's heart for meaningful relationships is vast. There is no way your husband or your children can ever provide the intimacy and relational satisfaction you need. A woman must have women friends. Do you have girlfriends? A best friend? Who are they?

What do you long for in your friendships?

If you don't have a close friendship with a woman you trust and enjoy, take a few minutes now and ask God to bring her into your life. Be like the stubborn widow and *keep* asking.

There is a fierce jealousy, a fiery devotion, and a great loyalty between women friends. Our friendships flow in the deep waters of the heart where God dwells and transformation takes place. Friendship is a great gift. How can you nurture, guard, and fight for your friendships?

Awkward Love

Let me say clearly, true friendship is *opposed*. One woman often feels less important or accused or needy or misunderstood to the other. Do you experience this?

Have you talked about it with your friend?

101

In our friendships, there will be times when we hurt or disappoint one another. It's inevitable in our broken world. But with the grace of God firmly holding us, reminding us that he is the source of our true happiness, it is possible to nurture and sustain deep friendships throughout our lives.

Ask God to reveal to you the truth that you are safe and secure in your relationship with him so you can risk being vulnerable with others and offer your true self.

Also ask God to help you become the kind of woman that others would long to have as a close friend. Ask him to reveal if there is anything hindering your friendships.

We long for friendships. Just like our God, we long for intimacy. Our desire for relationship is a part of our glory. And our deep longing is part of the grace given to Eve to drive her to the River of Life.

Go to him now. In prayer. In Desire. In Worship.

CHAPTER 11

Warrior Princesses

In God's name, we must fight them!

—JOAN OF ARC

Women are often portrayed in stories and tales as the "Damsel in Distress." We are the ones for whom men rise up and slay dragons. We are the "weaker sex." We are the ones waiting in our flowing gowns for the knight to come and carry us away on the back of his white horse. And yes, there are days when a knight in shining armor would be most welcome. We do long to be fought for, loved enough to be courageously protected. But there is a mighty fierceness set in the hearts of women by God. This fierceness is true to who we are and what we are created to do.

Women are warriors, too.

As always, let's ask for God's revelation and gentle guidance to come for us.

WOMEN ARE WARRIORS, TOO

Women are called to join in the Greatest Battle of all time—the battle being waged for the hearts of those around us. The human heart is the battlefield. The war is a deadly one; the results are devastating or glorious but always eternal. We are needed. There is much to be done. The hour is late. But we will only be victorious when we enter in with our feminine hearts—*when we battle as women.* What rises up in your heart, if anything, when you read that "We are needed"?

At this point, what does battling "as a woman" mean to you?

FIGHTING BACK

It is amazing what we will live with because we think it's normal when it absolutely is *not.* Is spiritual warfare a new category for you to think in?

Is it possible that you are struggling with something that may have its source in the spiritual realm? What?

EMOTIONAL ATTACKS

I know I am not alone in struggling with depression. Many women share this. Do you? If yes, how have you sought relief from it?

BODY, SOUL, AND SPIRIT

We human beings are made up of three interwoven parts. We are body, soul, and spirit. Each part affects the others in a mysterious interplay of life.

Our bodies may be out of balance due to a chemical imbalance or a need for more sleep, exercise, or better diets.

When we speak here of our souls, we are speaking of issues of our heart. We need to understand the story of our lives and receive the deep healing that God can bring.

Our spirit is that part of us in communion with God. We all carry real wounds. Demons are attracted to our unhealed wounds like sharks are attracted to blood in the water. That spiritual attack makes our pain much, much worse.

In what areas are you struggling? Body, soul, or spirit? How?

How may God be calling you to take a stand to fight for your freedom and healing?

We need to address all three aspects—body, soul, and spirit—in order to come more fully into healing. Far too many women will focus only on one or two aspects and not engage in the spiritual warfare that is swirling around us. But if we would be free, we must.

RELATIONAL ATTACKS

Another common enemy that often is at work in women's relationships is a spirit of accusation. In our friendships, in our relationships with peers at work, and especially in our marriages, we often feel that we are a disappointment to others. Do you experience this? What difficulties are you having right now in your relationships?

Have you considered that the enemy of your soul may have a hand in this?

It would be good to find out. Talk with your friend, your husband. Take a stand against the enemy's schemes, and command him to leave. Sometimes you have to be firm and pray several times. As Peter said, "firm in the faith" (1 Peter 5:9). But leave he does!

A WARRING BRIDE

Ladies, you are the Bride of Christ, and the Bride of Christ is a warring bride. We need to grow in our understanding and practice of spiritual warfare not only because we are being attacked, but because it is one of the primary ways that we grow in Christ. He uses spiritual warfare in our lives to strengthen our faith, to draw us closer to him, to train us for the roles we are meant to play, to encourage us to play those roles, and to prepare us for our future at his side.

It is *not* that we are alone. Christ will never leave us or forsake us. It is *not* even up to us. The battle is the Lord's.

Jesus has won the decisive victory against our Enemy. But we must apply it. Christianity is not a passive religion. We who are on the Lord's side must wield his victory. We must learn to enforce it. Women need to grow as warriors because we, too, were created to reign (see Genesis 1:26). And one day we will rule again (see Matthew 25:21; Revelation 22:5). Much of what God allows in your life is not for you to simply accept, but *to get you to rise up!*

What might that be in your life right now? A compulsion? A struggle with depression, fear, feeling overwhelmed?

Look up the following verses. (The Word of God is mighty in warfare. It is our sword!) What do they say?

1 John 3:8

Ephesians 6:10–17

Colossians 1:13–14

1 Timothy 6:12

Women are not meant to be helpless creatures. God has given us a fierceness that is holy and is to be used on behalf of others.

WARRIOR PRINCESSES

What does a warrior princess look like? Think Joan of Arc. Think Mother Teresa. Think Esther. Think Deborah. Think Mary, Jesus' mother. Women who were wise, cunning, strong, beautiful, courageous, victorious, and very present. Present to God, present to others, and present—aware of—themselves. Take a few minutes now and quiet your soul. Ask God to reveal the enemy's lies to you. What are they?

Are you able to identify the enemy's key lies to your heart? If not, continue to ask God for revelation. It is time to renounce those lies. Even if they still feel true. Stop agreeing with Satan's verdict on your life. Make all agreements with God. Ask God to speak the truth to you.

Women warriors are strong; yes, and they are also tender. There is mercy in them. There is vulnerability. In fact, offering a tender vulnerability can only be done by an incredibly strong woman rooted in Christ. Offering our hearts wisely, living in the freedom of God's love, inviting others to rest, alluring those in our lives to the heart of God, and responding to the heart of God in worship are some of the most powerful ways that a woman wars for her world. But she also puts on the full armor of God, daily, and takes her immovable stand against the powers of darkness.

Your life is a Love Story set in the midst of a life-and-death battle. The beauty, the adventure, the intimacy—they are what are most real. But it is a battle to gain them, and a battle to keep them. Jesus fights on your behalf and on behalf of those you love. He asks you to join him. Who would you love see come into God's kingdom?

Who do you want to see released to take their place in God's kingdom and fulfill his call on their lives?

What do *you* long to be free of?

Then you must take spiritual warfare seriously. First on behalf of your own heart and then mightily, for those you love.

Let's come to God in prayer:

Dearest Jesus, thank you for ransoming me. Father, thank you for rescuing me from the domain of darkness and transferring me into the kingdom of the Son you love. I am grateful beyond words to be yours. Please strengthen me for battle. Please reveal to me when I am under spiritual attack and teach me to take a stand against the enemy and to resist him. Even today, Jesus. In the name of Jesus Christ. Amen.

CHAPTER 12

An Irreplaceable Role

Mary responded, "I am the Lord's servant, and I am willing
to accept whatever he wants. May everything you have said come true."

—LUKE 1:38 NLT

The story of *Cinderella* turns upon an invitation. *Our* story turns upon invitation. The King of kings invites us to choose him, to continue choosing him above all others and to risk joining him in the Great Dance, to offer what we have to offer, to live by faith, hope, and love, and to play the irreplaceable, larger-than-we-are-comfortable-with role that is ours to play. Take a moment to pray before you go any farther in this chapter.

Finding our place in God's story (which is what we mean by finding your calling) is a process of discovery. We believe that God writes the destiny of our lives upon our hearts—in the form of our dreams and desires.

Uncovering those desires and dreams—and recovering ones that have been lost—is a crucial part to finding our place in God's story. God will send us all sorts of things to stir us to remember. As you let yourself dream and wonder, recall those things that have stirred your heart—memories, photographs, stories and movies and characters you most deeply love, identify with, long to be. Then ask God why—ask him to speak to you about that.

INVITED

How gracious that God comes to us with invitation. As a woman, you don't need to arrange; you don't need to make it happen. You only need to respond. Do you have a sense of what it is that God is inviting you to? What?

Mary, the mother of Jesus' life, also turned upon invitation. What was God's invitation to Mary? How did she respond?

The invitations of our Prince come to us in all sorts of ways. Your heart itself, as a woman, is an invitation. . . .Your Lover has written something on your heart. It is a call to find a life of Romance and to protect that love affair as your most precious treasure. His invitation is a call to cultivate the beauty you hold inside and to unveil your beauty on behalf of others. And it is a call to adventure, to become the *ezer* the world desperately needs you to be. Are you beginning to believe that you possess a beauty to unveil? A beauty the world needs?

The Power of a Woman's Life

When the history of the world is finally told rightly—one of the great joys when we reach the Wedding Feast of the Lamb—it will be as clear as day that women have been essential to every great move of God upon this earth. Can you think of some that we did not mention? Biblically? Historically?

From the beginning, Eve was God's gift to the world—his *ezer kenegdo* for us. History is still unfolding and your existence on this earth as a woman is proof that you have an irreplaceable role to play. Your feminine heart is an invitation by your Creator to play an irreplaceable role in his Story. Isn't that what your Lover wrote there? Some dream, some desire. What has God written on your heart? What dreams, what desires, what longings?

Your Irreplaceable Role

Our true places as women in God's Story are as diverse and unique as wildflowers in a field. But we all share certain spheres of influence to which we are called to be an *ezer* in our relationships, in the body of Christ, and in the world.

We learn from the Trinity that relationship is the most important thing in the universe. You have an irreplaceable role in your relationships. Who are the key people in your relationships?

What does it look like for you to offer your beauty, your fierce devotion, and your love in relationships?

How do they need you to be their *ezer*? What would keep you from offering it to them?

Do your relationships feel *opposed* at times? How? Who do you want to fight for?

Your life is also part of a larger movement, a mystical fellowship, the kingdom of God advancing here on earth. The fellowship of Christ is messy, because it, too, is *opposed*. And here, you have an irreplaceable role to play.

We haven't time here to address the issues surrounding "the proper role of women" in the church. However, we do believe it is far more helpful to start with Design—with what God designed a woman to be and to offer. God desires that wherever and however you offer yourself to the body of Christ, you'll have the protection of good men over you. Issues of headship and authority are intended for the *benefit* of women, not their suppression. Do you know your gifting? Your calling? What is it?

When we speak of your irreplaceable role within the body of Christ, we're talking about the true fellowship of those whose hearts are captured for Jesus, who have become his intimate allies. You want to offer yourself to those who thirst for what you have. If it's not wanted where you are, ask Jesus what he wants you to do. If you are called, God will make a way. Either where you are or through a change of circumstances. Follow your Lover; respond to his invitations. With him, there is no stopping you. Do you need to change your situation—find a true fellowship where your heart is wanted—and where you are among those who want what you want?

Stepping further out into your farthest sphere of influence, you have something essential to offer the World. It may be in the form of a notable career. It may be a hidden life, well-lived. Some women are called to the marketplace. How is God calling you to play your irreplaceable role there?

The crucial issue is this: It is as a *woman* you must live there. Do not be naive. The World is still deeply marred by the Fall. The Evil One holds sway over the World and its systems. In the World you must be as cunning as a Rahab, an Esther, a Tamar. You must walk wisely. You must not let them shape you into their view of what a woman is. You'll end up a man. What you have to offer is as a woman. Uniquely feminine. If you have a role in the marketplace, what would it look like for you to recover more of your feminine heart there?

WHAT IS WRITTEN ON YOUR HEART?

God's invitations ultimately are matters of the heart. They come through our passions, those desires set deep within us. How have God's invitations come to you in the past?

How are they coming to you now?

As God restores your heart and sets you free, you will recover long-lost passions, long-forsaken dreams. Those emerging desires are invitations to bring your heart to your Lover and ask him to clarify, to deepen, to speak to you about how and when and with whom. What desires are emerging within you? Any long-lost passions being rekindled?

DO NOT GIVE WAY TO FEAR

Responding to the invitations of Jesus often feels like the riskiest thing we've ever done. The life of the friends of God is a life of profound risk. The risk of playing the irreplaceable role that is ours to play. Of course it is hard. If it were easy, you'd see lots of women living this way. The reason we fear to step out is because we know that it might not go well. What is it you fear most?

How can we live lives without fear (1 Peter 2:21–23)?

What is God calling you to offer?

God invites us to share and give in our weaknesses. He wants us to offer the beauty that he has given us even when we are keenly aware that it is not all that we wish it were. He wants us to trust him. How it turns out is no longer the point. Living in this way, as a woman alive, is a choice we make because it is the woman we want to be. It is our loving response to our Lover's invitation.

Be Present

Life is a tenuous thing—fragile, fleeting. Don't wait for tomorrow. Be here now! Where would it be good for you to be more *present?* To offer your presence?

To live as an authentic, ransomed, and redeemed woman means to be real and present, in this moment. What have we to offer, really, other than who we are and what God has been pouring into our lives? It was not by accident that you were born; it was not by chance that you have the desires you do. The Victorious Trinity has planned on your being here now, "for such as time as this" (Esth. 4:14 NKJV). We need you.

118

Jesus knew who he was. God wants you to know who you are as well. So, who *are* you? How does God see you?

Is he captivated by your beauty?

Does he love you?

What is he inviting you to?

Jesus is extending his hand to you. He asks, "May I have this dance every day of your life?" He is captivated by your beauty. He is smiling. He cares nothing of the opinion of others. He is standing. He will lead. He waits for your response. What is your heart's response to Jesus?

There is always more. More healing. More life. More repentance. More freedom. More of Jesus. More faith, more hope, more love. And dear sister, that is very good news. We are on this journey together. A journey with Jesus to become increasingly transformed into his beautiful likeness; increasingly *his*.

Rest in his love. He is enough.